G000046670

KS2
8–9
Years

Master Maths at Home

Extra Challenges

Scan the QR code to help your child's learning at home.

 | **MATHS** **NO PROBLEM!**

mastermathsathome.com

How to use this book

Maths — No Problem! created **Master Maths at Home** to help children develop fluency in the subject and a rich understanding of core concepts.

Key features of the Master Maths at Home books include:

- Carefully designed lessons that provide structure, but also allow flexibility in how they're used.

- Speech bubbles containing content designed to spark diverse conversations, with many discussion points that don't have obvious 'right' or 'wrong' answers.

- Rich illustrations that will guide children to a discussion of shapes and units of measurement, allowing them to make connections to the wider world around them.

- Exercises that allow a flexible approach and can be adapted to suit any child's cognitive or functional ability.

- Clearly laid-out pages that encourage children to practise a range of higher-order skills.

- A community of friendly and relatable characters who introduce each lesson and come along as your child progresses through the series.

You can see more guidance on how to use these books at **mastermathsathome.com**.

We're excited to share all the ways you can learn maths!

Copyright © 2022 Maths — No Problem!

Maths — No Problem!
mastermathsathome.com
www.mathsnoproblem.com
hello@mathsnoproblem.com

First published in Great Britain in 2022 by
Dorling Kindersley Limited
One Embassy Gardens, 8 Viaduct Gardens, London SW11 7BW
A Penguin Random House Company

The authorised representative in the EEA is Dorling Kindersley
Verlag GmbH. Arnulfstr. 124, 80636 Munich, Germany

10 9 8 7 6 5 4 3 2 1
001–327093–Jan/22

All rights reserved. Without limiting the rights under the copyright reserved above, no part of this publication may be reproduced, stored in, or introduced into a retrieval system, or transmitted, in any form, or by any means (electronic, mechanical, photocopying, recording, or otherwise), without the prior written permission of the copyright owner.

A CIP catalogue record for this book is available from the British Library.

ISBN: 978-0-24153-938-5
Printed and bound in the UK

For the curious
www.dk.com

MIX
Paper from
responsible sources
FSC™ C018179

This book was made with Forest Stewardship Council™ certified paper - one small step in DK's commitment to a sustainable future. For more information go to www.dk.com/our-green-pledge

Acknowledgements
The publisher would like to thank the authors and consultants Andy Psarianos, Judy Hornigold, Adam Gifford and Dr Anne Hermanson.

The Castledown typeface has been used with permission from the Colophon Foundry.

Contents

Ruby   Elliott   Amira   Charles   Lulu   Sam   Oak   Holly   Ravi   Emma   Jacob   Hannah

Comparing and ordering decimals

Starter

Which number is greater?

35.1   35.09

Example

35.1 is 3 tens, 5 ones and 1 tenth.

tens	ones	tenths	hundredths
3	5	1	0

35.09 is 3 tens, 5 ones and 9 hundredths.

tens	ones	tenths	hundredths
3	5	0	9

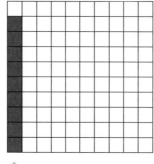

The square is made up of 1 hundred equal size pieces. Each piece is 1 hundredth of the square.

35.1 is 1 hundredth more than 35.09.

$\dfrac{1}{10} = \dfrac{10}{100}$ $\dfrac{9}{100}$

1 tenth is greater than 9 hundredths.

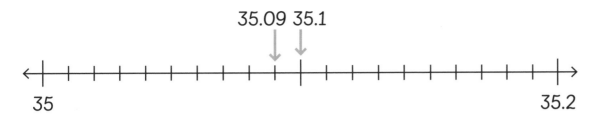

35.1 is greater than 35.09.

Practice

1 Circle the greater number.

(a)   12.55   12.6   (b)   87.99   88

(c)   10.01   10.10   (d)   90.95   95.09

2 (a) Use these digits to make 4 numbers, each with 2 decimal places.

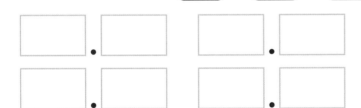

(b) Put your numbers in order from smallest to greatest.

[   ] , [   ] , [   ] , [   ]

3 [   ] is 0.03 more than 2.5 and 0.02 less than 2.55.

Rounding decimals

Round these masses to estimate the total mass of the three cases.

 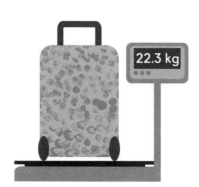 

Example

Round 22.7 kg to the nearest kg.

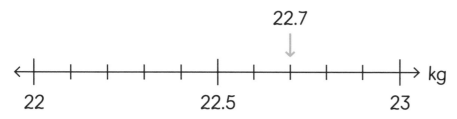

22.7 is nearer to 23 than to 22.
22.7 kg is approximately 23 kg (to the nearest kg).
22.7 kg ≈ 23 kg

Round 22.3 kg to the nearest kg.

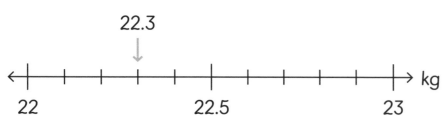 

22.3 kg ≈ 22 kg

22.3 is nearer to 22 than to 23.
22.3 kg is approximately 22 kg (to the nearest kg).

Round 35.5 kg to the nearest kg.

35.5

35.5 is exactly halfway between 35 and 36.

35   35.5   36

We take 35.5 kg to be approximately 36 kg to the nearest kg.

35.5 kg ≈ 36 kg

22 kg + 23 kg + 36 kg = 81 kg

The total mass of the three cases is approximately 81 kg.

Practice

1 Round these decimals to the nearest kg.

(a) 46.9 kg ≈ _____ kg   (b) 25.1 kg ≈ _____ kg

(c) 44.5 kg ≈ _____ kg

2 Estimate the total length of these strips of ribbon when rounded to the nearest cm.

(a)

12.7 cm ≈ _____ cm

(b)

15.2 cm ≈ _____ cm

The total length of both strips of ribbon is approximately _____ cm.

Writing fractions as decimals

Starter

How can we write these fractions as decimals?

$$\frac{1}{2} \qquad \frac{1}{4} \qquad \frac{3}{10}$$

Example

We write 3 tenths as 0.3.

$$\frac{3}{10} = 0.3$$

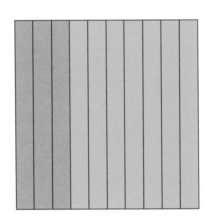

$$\frac{3}{10} = 3 \text{ tenths}$$

$$\frac{1}{2} = 5 \text{ tenths}$$

$$\times 5$$
$$\frac{1}{2} = \frac{5}{10}$$
$$\times 5$$

We write 5 tenths as 0.5.

$$\frac{1}{2} = 0.5$$

$$\frac{1}{2} = \frac{5}{10}$$

$$= 0.5$$

$\frac{1}{4}$ = 25 hundredths

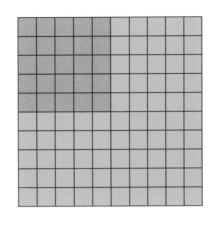

$\times 25$

$\frac{1}{4} = \frac{25}{100}$

$\times 25$

$\frac{1}{4} = \frac{25}{100}$

= 0.25

We write 25 hundredths as 0.25.

$\frac{1}{4}$ = 0.25

Practice

1 Write these fractions as decimals.

(a) $\frac{4}{10}$ = [ ] tenths = [ ]

(b) $\frac{3}{4}$ = [ ] hundredths = [ ]

(c) $\frac{2}{5}$ = [ ] tenths = [ ]

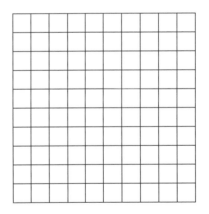

2 Write these amounts as decimals.

(a) $6\frac{7}{10}$ kg = [ ] kg

(b) $3\frac{1}{2}$ cm = [ ] cm

(c) $2\frac{1}{4}$ km = [ ] km

(d) $7\frac{4}{5}$ kg = [ ] kg

9

Dividing whole numbers by 100

Starter

18 l of paint is poured into 100 identical paint pots. How much paint is in each pot?

Paint

18 l

Example

Divide 10 and 8 by 100.

What is 10 divided by 100?

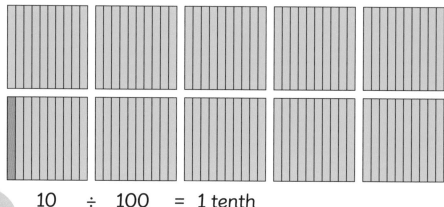

$$10 \div 100 = 1 \text{ tenth}$$
$$= 0.1$$

1 tenth is 100 times smaller than 10.

digit 1 in tens place

digit 1 in tenths place

1 tenth is 1 tenth of one paint pot.

When 10 is divided by 100, the 1 in the tens place becomes 1 in the tenths place.

What is 8 divided by 100?

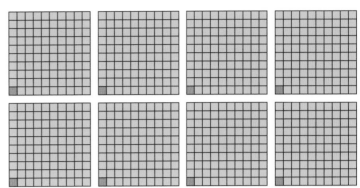

8 hundredths is 100 times smaller than 8.

$8 \div 100 = 0.08$

When 8 is divided by 100, the 8 in the ones place becomes 8 in the hundredths place.

1☐ is 1 hundredth of one paint pot.

tens	ones	tenths	hundredths		tens	ones	tenths	hundredths
1	8 .			÷ 100 →		0 .	1	8

$18 \div 100 = 0.18$

There is 0.18 l of paint in each pot.

When I look at it in a place value chart I can see what happens when I divide a number by 100.

Practice

Divide.

 1 $9 \div 10 =$

 2 $9 \div 100 =$

 3 $11 \div 10 =$

4 $11 \div 100 =$

5 $80 \div 10 =$

6 $80 \div 100 =$

Adding using mental strategies

Starter

Amira's dad needs to buy a new piano and an electric guitar for his band. The piano he likes costs £4999 and the electric guitar costs £1999.

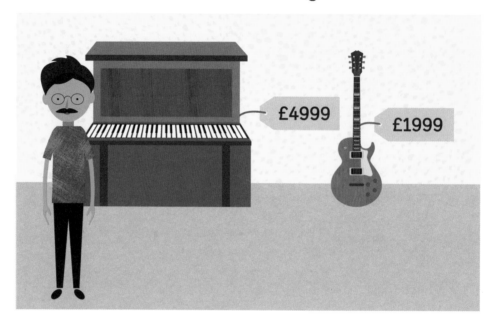

£4999

£1999

How much will Amira's dad pay if he buys the two musical instruments?

Example

We need to find the sum of 1999 and 4999 to get the total cost.

We can add them this way.

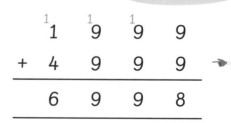

```
  ¹1  ¹9  ¹9   9
+  4   9   9   9
   6   9   9   8
```

There is an easier way. We can add 1 to 1999 and 1 to 4999.

$1999 + 1 = 2000$

$4999 + 1 = 5000$

I already know the sum. $2000 + 5000 = 7000$

We must not forget to remove the 2 that we added to find the correct sum. $7000 - 2 = 6998$

If Amira's dad buys the two musical instruments he will pay £6998.

Practice

Add using mental strategies.

1   (a) $2345 + 10 =$ ☐   (b) $100 + 587 =$ ☐

      $2345 + 9 =$ ☐ $99 + 587 =$ ☐

     (c) $3269 + 500 =$ ☐   (d) $4231 + 4000 =$ ☐

      $3269 + 499 =$ ☐ $4231 + 3998 =$ ☐

2   (a) $999 + 2999 =$ ☐   (b) $999 + 3001 =$ ☐

     (c) $5997 + 998 =$ ☐   (d) $3998 + 5998 =$ ☐

Subtracting using mental strategies

Starter

Amira's dad cannot spend £6998 on musical instruments as it is too much money. The shopkeeper tells him that if he buys second-hand instruments he will save £2999.

How much will Amira's dad pay if he buys the second-hand musical instruments?

Example

We can use this method to find the cost of the second-hand instruments. I know this method always works.

$$
\begin{array}{r}
\overset{5}{\cancel{6}}\ \overset{18}{\cancel{9}}\ \overset{18}{\cancel{9}}\ \overset{18}{\cancel{8}} \\
-\ 2\ \ 9\ \ 9\ \ 9 \\
\hline
3\ \ 9\ \ 9\ \ 9 \\
\hline
\end{array}
$$

There is an easier way. We can add 1 to both numbers so we can easily subtract.

6998 + 1 = 6999

2999 + 1 = 3000

14

When we add the same amount to both numbers, the difference remains the same.

We can subtract 3000 from 6999 easily.
6999 – 3000 = 3999

We can also use a number line to help us find the difference.

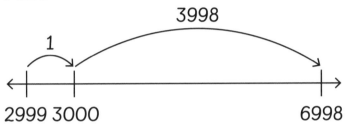

3998

1

2999 3000   6998

$3000 - 2999 = 1$
$6998 - 3000 = 3998$
$1 + 3998 = 3999$

Amira's dad will pay £3999 if he buys the second-hand musical instruments.

Practice

Subtract using mental strategies.

1 (a) $43 - 19 =$

(b) $101 - 99 =$

(c) $803 - 198 =$

(d) $1000 - 326 =$

(e) $5000 - 1674 =$

(f) $9008 - 99 =$

2 (a) $1001 - 999 =$

(b) $1001 - 199 =$

(c) $700 - 675 =$

(d) $1700 - 1575 =$

15

Addition and subtraction

Starter

A garden centre has 1285 tulip bulbs and 3634 daffodil bulbs. It sells 468 tulip bulbs and 1532 daffodil bulbs.
How many bulbs are left at the garden centre altogether?

Example

We can add both types of bulbs together to find the total amount of bulbs they started with.

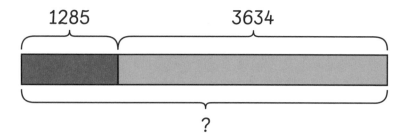

?

$$
\begin{array}{r}
1\ {}^{1}2\ 8\ 5 \\
+\ 3\ 6\ 3\ 4 \\
\hline
4\ 9\ 1\ 9
\end{array}
$$

We can find the sum of the bulbs they sold by adding 468 to 1532.

The garden centre started with 4919 bulbs altogether.

468 + 1532 can be added like this. The garden centre sold 2000 bulbs in total.

468 + 32 = 500
500 + 1500 = 2000
468 + 1532 = 2000

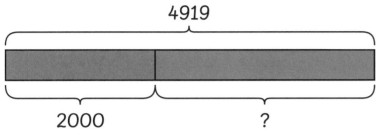

Now we can subtract the number of bulbs they sold from the number of bulbs they started with.

4919

2000   ?

4919 − 2000 = 2919

There are 2919 bulbs left at the garden centre.

Practice

In one day, a baker bakes 396 white bread rolls.
He bakes 129 more brown bread rolls than white bread rolls.

1 How many brown bread rolls rolls does he bake?

He bakes ☐ brown bread rolls.

2 How many bread rolls does he bake altogether?

He bakes ☐ bread rolls altogether.

3 A supermarket buys half of the white bread rolls and 500 brown bread rolls. Altogether, how many bread rolls are left over?

Altogether, ☐ bread rolls are left over.

Multiplying 3-digit numbers

Starter

A sack of rice weighs 3 times as much as a small bag of rice.
How much do 1 sack and 2 small bags of rice weigh?

Rice
454 g

Example

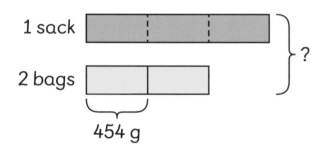

1 sack

2 bags

?

454 g

One bag of rice weighs 454 g.

The sack of rice weighs 3 times as much as one bag.

To find the total weight, we need to multiply 454 by 5.

$$
\begin{array}{r}
{}^2\!4\ \ {}^2\!5\ \ 4 \\
\times \quad\quad 5 \\
\hline
2\ \ 2\ \ 7\ \ 0
\end{array}
$$

425 × 5 = 2270
They weigh 2270 g.

1000 g is equal to 1 kg, so 2270 g is equal to 2.27 kg.

The sack and the 2 bags of rice weigh 2.27 kg.

1 Find the product.

(a) 123 × 4 = ☐

(b) 333 × 9 = ☐

(c) 835 × 6 = ☐

(d) 799 × 7 = ☐

2 Find an equation that gives a product that is more than 500 and less than 700.

☐ × ☐ = ☐

3 Emma played a video game 3 days in a row. On Tuesday Emma scored half as many points as she did on Monday. On Wednesday she scored 3 times as many points as she did on Tuesday. She scored 225 points on Tuesday.

How many points did she score in total over the 3 days?

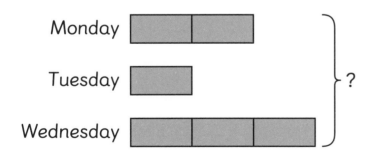

Emma scored ☐ points in total over the 3 days.

Dividing 3-digit numbers

Starter

120 children are put into 8 equal groups.
How many children are in each group?

Example

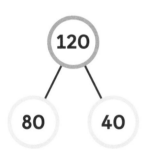

120

80   40

We can split 120 up to make it easier to divide by 8.

Both 80 and 40 are easy to divide by 8.

$80 \div 8 = 10$
$40 \div 8 = 5$

$120 \div 8 = 15$
There are 15 children in each group.

Practice

1 Find the quotient.

(a) 168 ÷ 4 = [ ]

(b) 861 ÷ 3 = [ ]

(c) 545 ÷ 5 = [ ]

(d) 918 ÷ 6 = [ ]

2 £119 is shared equally between 7 people.
How much money does each person get?

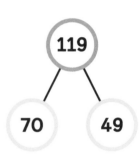

[ ]

Each person gets £ [ ] .

3 A pastry chef needs to put 864 tarts into boxes of 8 tarts.
How many boxes will he need?

[ ]

The pastry chef needs [ ] boxes.

Dividing 3-digit numbers with remainder

Starter

The shopkeeper packs 210 apricots equally into bags.
He fills each bag with 8 apricots.
How many bags can he fill?
How many apricots will be left over?

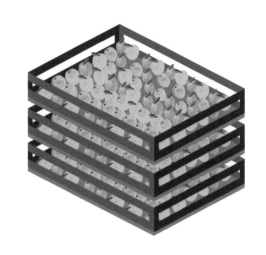

Example

We need to divide 210 by 8.

We can split 210 into 160, 48 and 2.

$160 \div 8 = 20$

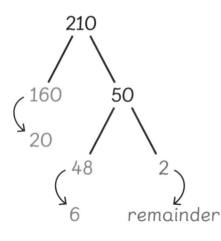

210
160   50
20
48   2
6   remainder

$48 \div 8 = 6$

We cannot divide 2 apricots by 8 so we will have 2 apricots left over.

We then add the two quotients and show the remainder.

$20 + 6 = 26$ remainder 2

$210 \div 8 = 26$ remainder 2

We can also use long division.

```
          2   6
    8 )   2   1   0
       -  1   6          ⟶   20 × 8 = 160
          5   0
       -      4   8       ⟶   6 × 8 = 48
              2          ⟶   remainder
```

$210 \div 8 = 26$ remainder 2

The shopkeeper can fill 26 bags. There will be 2 apricots left over.

Practice

1 Find the quotient and the remainder.

(a) $200 \div 7 =$

(b) $314 \div 6 =$

(c) $567 \div 8 =$

2 Six classes of children share 179 pencils equally.

(a) How many pencils does each class receive?

Each class receives ☐ pencils.

(b) How many pencils are left over?

☐ pencils are left over.

Multiplication and division

Starter

A shopowner receives a small box and a large box, both containing phone covers.

The small box contains 84 phone covers. The large box contains 4 times as many phone covers as the small box.

If all these phone covers are repackaged into packs of 4, how many packs of 4 can the shopowner make?

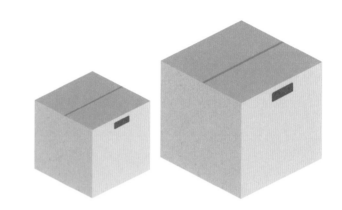

Example

First we need to find the total number of phone covers.

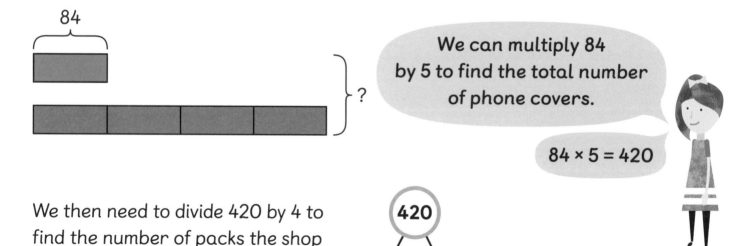

84

?

We can multiply 84 by 5 to find the total number of phone covers.

$84 \times 5 = 420$

We then need to divide 420 by 4 to find the number of packs the shop can make. We can split 420 into 400 and 20.

420

400   20

$420 \div 4 = 105$

The shopowner can make 105 packs of 4 phone covers.

1 There are twice as many children as adults at a water park.
There are 128 adults at the water park.
Half of the people at the water park are wearing goggles.
How many people are not wearing goggles?

_____ people are not wearing goggles.

2 Lulu has 3 times as many blue beads as red beads.
She has twice as many green beads as red beads.
Lulu has 85 red beads.
She makes necklaces that have 30 beads each.
How many necklaces can Lulu make?

Lulu can make _____ necklaces.

Simplifying improper fractions

Starter

A bakery has $2\frac{1}{2}$ cakes. If the baker cuts $\frac{1}{8}$ of a cake for one slice, how many slices can she cut?

 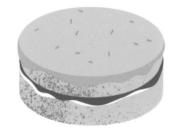 

Example

Each slice is 1 eighth of a cake.

Each whole cake is 8 slices. One half of a cake is 4 slices.

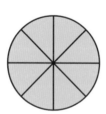 + 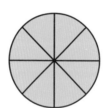 +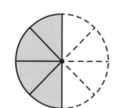

8 eighths + 8 eighths + 4 eighths = 20 eighths

$$2\frac{1}{2} = \frac{20}{8}$$

If the baker cuts the slices as eighths she can cut 20 slices from $2\frac{1}{2}$ cakes.

We can add all the slices.
8 + 8 + 4 = 20
There are 20 eighths in total.

26

1 A cafe has two $5\frac{1}{2}$ l bottles of tomato ketchup.

The waiters need to fill $\frac{3}{4}$ l bottles to put on the tables.

How many $\frac{3}{4}$ l bottles can they fill?

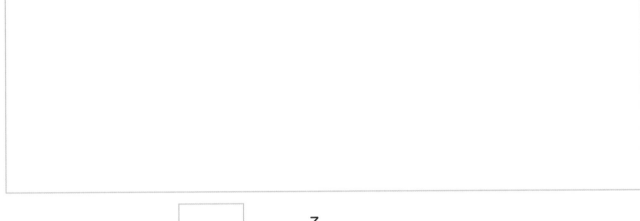

The waiters can fill ☐ of the $\frac{3}{4}$ l bottles.

2 Each customer is given $\frac{2}{5}$ of a whole pizza.

How many customers can the restaurant serve if it has $4\frac{4}{5}$ pizzas?

The restaurant can serve ☐ customers from $4\frac{4}{5}$ pizzas.

Adding fractions

Starter

A cafe has these pieces left from two cakes of the same size.
What is the total amount of cake left?

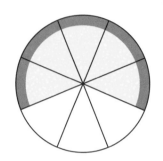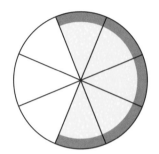

Example

Both cakes have $\frac{5}{8}$ remaining.
We can add $\frac{5}{8}$ to $\frac{5}{8}$ to find out the total amount of cake left.

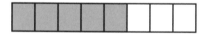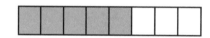

5 eighths   +   5 eighths   =   10 eighths

If I move the pieces from one cake to complete the other cake I can see how much is left.

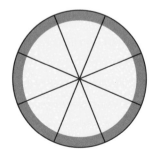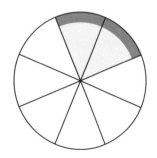

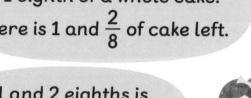

There is 1 whole cake and 2 pieces. Each piece is 1 eighth of a whole cake.
There is 1 and $\frac{2}{8}$ of cake left.

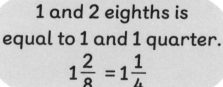

1 and 2 eighths is equal to 1 and 1 quarter.
$1\frac{2}{8} = 1\frac{1}{4}$

There are $1\frac{1}{4}$ cakes left in total.

Practice

1 Add and write as a mixed number.

(a) $\dfrac{3}{4} + \dfrac{3}{4} = 1$ ☐

(b) $\dfrac{5}{8} + \dfrac{7}{8} = 1$ ☐

(c) $\dfrac{9}{10} + \dfrac{7}{10} =$ ☐

(d) $3\dfrac{4}{5} + 4\dfrac{3}{5} =$ ☐

2 Sam has $\dfrac{7}{9}$ of one bar of chocolate.

Jacob has $\dfrac{5}{9}$ of the same type of chocolate bar.

How much chocolate do the two boys have altogether?

The two boys have ☐ chocolate bars altogether.

3 Charles has two strips of ribbon. One is $2\dfrac{5}{6}$ m and the other is $3\dfrac{1}{2}$ m.

What is the total length of ribbon that Charles has?

Charles has ☐ m of ribbon in total.

Subtracting fractions

Starter

Hannah is baking a pie. She has $2\frac{1}{5}$ kg of sugar.

She puts $\frac{3}{5}$ kg of the sugar in the pie.

What is the mass of the sugar Hannah has left?

Example

2 and 1 fifth is equal to 11 fifths.
I can subtract 3 fifths from 11 fifths.
$11 - 3 = 8$
There are 8 fifths left.

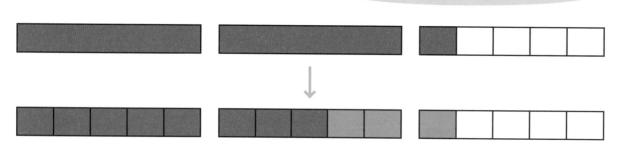

8 fifths is equal to 1 and 3 fifths.
$\frac{8}{5} = 1\frac{3}{5}$

Hannah has $1\frac{3}{5}$ kg of sugar left.

1 Emma has $2\frac{1}{4}$ l of water in a jug.

She uses $\frac{3}{4}$ l to make some squash.

How much water is left in the jug?

  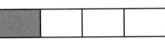

There is [ ] l of water left in the jug.

2 There is $3\frac{1}{6}$ l of paint in a can.

Oak's dad uses $\frac{2}{3}$ l to paint a wall.

What is the volume of paint left in the can?

There is [ ] l of paint left in the can.

Finding amounts using fractions

Starter

Lulu has 2 l of milk. She uses $\frac{1}{3}$ l to make a milkshake and pours the rest equally into 5 identical glasses.

How much milk is in each glass?

Example

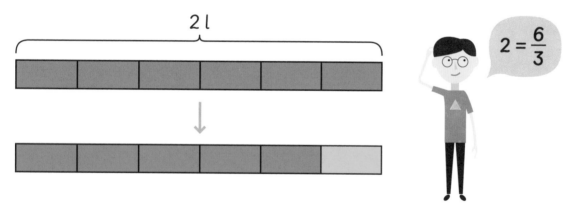

2 l

$2 = \frac{6}{3}$

There are 6 thirds in 2.

$$\frac{6}{3} - \frac{1}{3} = \frac{5}{3}$$

There are 5 thirds left.

Each glass has $\frac{1}{3}$ l of milk.

1 Sam has a 3 kg bag of rice.

He uses $\frac{3}{4}$ kg and then stores the remaining rice in $\frac{1}{4}$ kg bags.

How many $\frac{1}{4}$ kg bags of rice does Sam have?

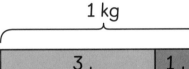

Sam has ⬚ $\frac{1}{4}$ kg bags of rice.

2 Emma has $2\frac{1}{4}$ l of pineapple juice. She uses $1\frac{1}{8}$ l to make a smoothie.

What is the volume of pineapple juice that Emma has left?

Emma has ⬚ l of pineapple juice left.

3 Jacob has 2 cakes. He eats $\frac{1}{3}$ of one cake and shares the remaining cake

equally between 10 friends.

How much cake will each friend get?

Each friend will get ⬚ of cake.

Finding durations of time

It takes Ravi 20 minutes to walk from home to the cinema. He stays at the cinema for 85 minutes. He then walks home and arrives back at 18:20.

At what time did Ravi leave home to go to the cinema?

Example

20 min + 85 min + 20 min = 125 min

125 = 60 + 60 + 5
125 min = 2 h 5 min

60 min = 1 h

16:15 is quarter past 4 in the afternoon.

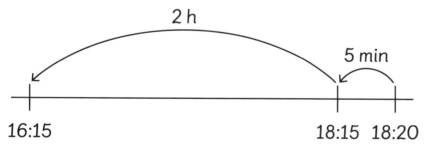

2 h

5 min

16:15

18:15 18:20

Ravi left home at 16:15.

1 A bus journey usually takes 105 minutes, but the bus is delayed on the journey by half an hour.
It finally arrives at its destination at 21:40.
At what time did the bus journey start?

The bus journey started at ____ .

2 Oak leaves home at 12:35 p.m.
She returns at quarter to 4 in the afternoon.
How long was Oak away from home?

Oak was away from home for ____ h ____ min.

3 It takes 50 minutes for Amira to travel to the shopping centre.
She wants to shop for 45 minutes and take another 30 minutes for lunch.
She needs to be home by 17:50.
At what time does Amira need to leave home for the shopping centre?

Amira needs to leave home for the shopping centre at ____ .

Measuring area

Starter

Elliott puts his book down on Jacob's drawing.
Is it still possible to find the area of the rectangle that Jacob drew?

= 1 square unit

Example

There are 9 square units in each row.

I know there are 5 rows.

9 × 5 = 45

It is still possible to find the area of the rectangle. It is 45 square units.

Find the area of each of these rectangles before the corners were cut off.

[ ] = 1 square unit

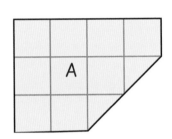

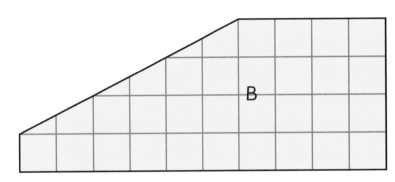

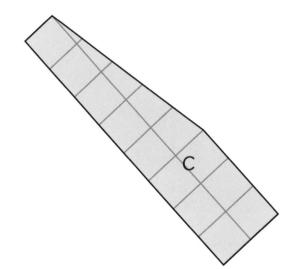

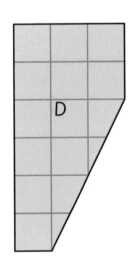

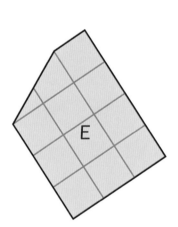

1 Area of A = [ ] square units **2** Area of B = [ ] square units

3 Area of C = [ ] square units **4** Area of D = [ ] square units

5 Area of E = [ ] square units

37

Estimating amounts of money

Starter

What is the total cost of these 4 items when rounded to the nearest £?

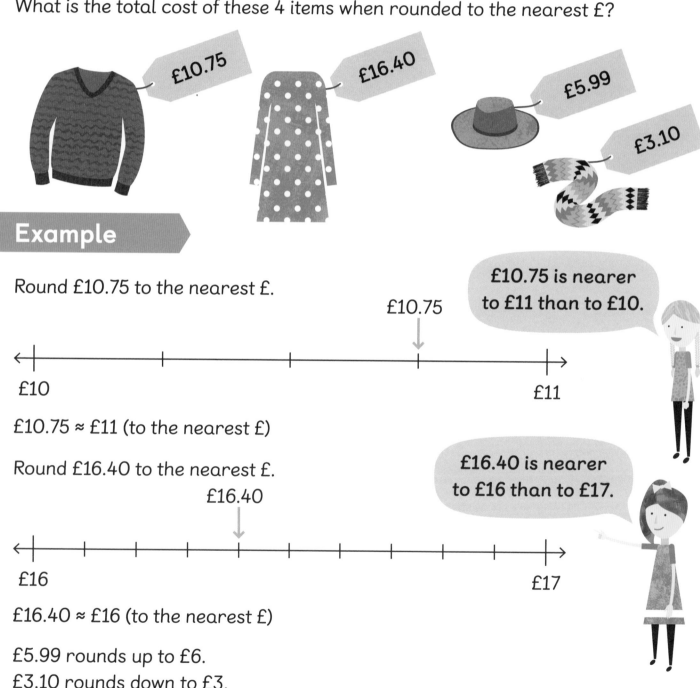

£10.75

£16.40

£5.99

£3.10

Example

Round £10.75 to the nearest £.

£10.75 is nearer to £11 than to £10.

£10.75

£10

£11

£10.75 ≈ £11 (to the nearest £)

Round £16.40 to the nearest £.

£16.40 is nearer to £16 than to £17.

£16.40

£16

£17

£16.40 ≈ £16 (to the nearest £)

£5.99 rounds up to £6.
£3.10 rounds down to £3.
£11 + £16 + £6 + £3 = £36

The total cost of the 4 items is £36 when rounded to the nearest £.

1 Estimate the total cost of these items by rounding to the nearest £.

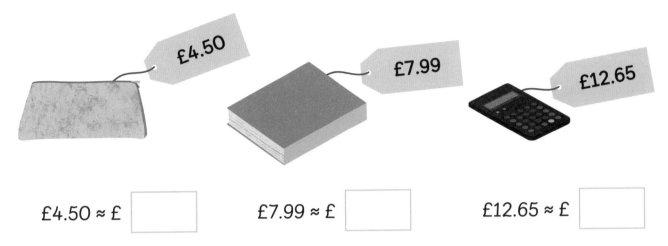

£4.50 ≈ £ [ ]   £7.99 ≈ £ [ ]   £12.65 ≈ £ [ ]

The total cost of these items is £ [ ] (to the nearest £).

2 (a) Estimate the total cost of the meal by rounding to the nearest £.

Yum Yum Tasty Restaurant

Fish and chips	£8.90
Cheese toastie	£5.50
Chicken curry	£10.10
Salmon salad	£15.55
Ice cream	£4.00
4 Milkshakes	£16.80

Total Cost

The total cost of the meal is £ [ ] (rounded to the nearest £).

(b) Which item did not need to be rounded? [ ]

Making symmetrical figures

Starter

Charles is making some prints.

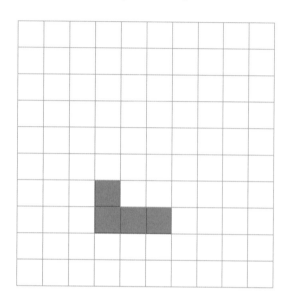 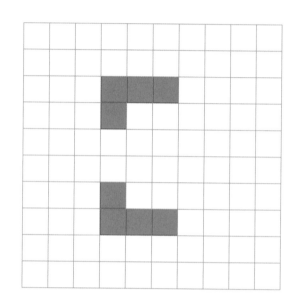

Where did he fold the paper to make this symmetrical print?

Example

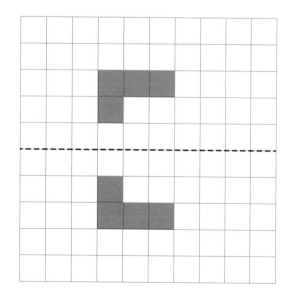 

This is the line of symmetry.

Charles folded the paper along the dashed line to make this symmetrical figure.

Charles made some more prints using red paint. Draw the lines of symmetry that show how Charles folded each piece of paper on the left to make the symmetrical shapes on the right.

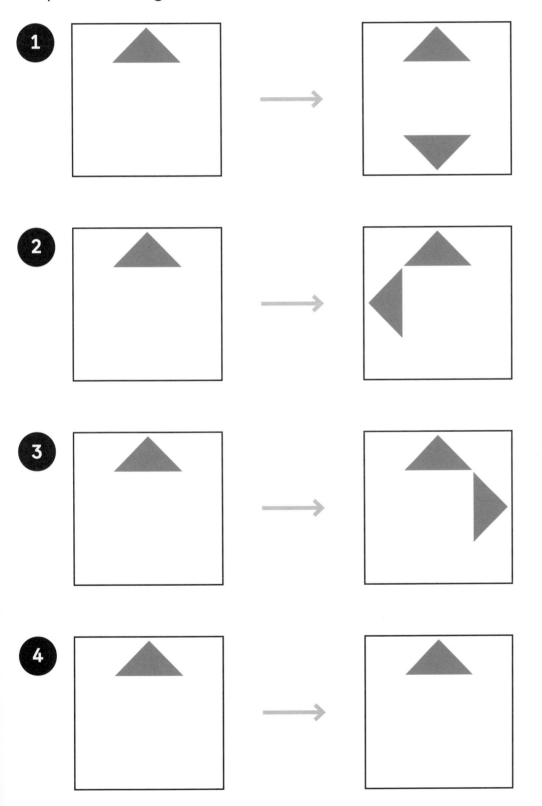

Describing movement

Starter

How can we move shape PQRS so that Q moves to (5,5)?

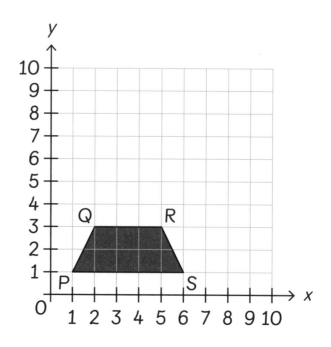

Example

We can move shape PQRS in two different ways so that Q ends up at (5,5).

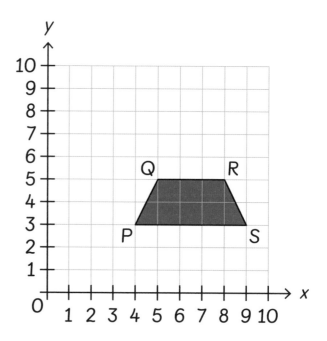

The shape translates 2 units up and then 3 units to the right.
The shape can also translate 3 units to the right and then 2 units up.

1

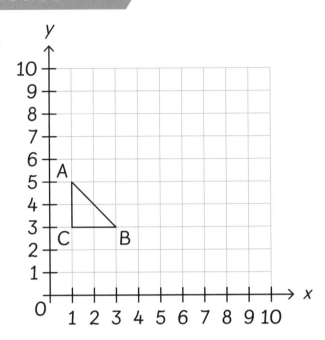

Describe the translation using up, down, left and right, that moves:

(a) B to (2,2) ☐ unit(s) ☐ , ☐ unit(s) ☐

(b) A to (4,6) ☐ unit(s) ☐ , ☐ unit(s) ☐

(c) C to (2,5) ☐ unit(s) ☐ , ☐ unit(s) ☐

2 (a) Draw a triangle with the following coordinates: A (3,6), B (3,4), C (5,4).

(b) Translate the triangle 1 unit right and then 3 units up.

(c) Write the coordinates after the translation.

A (☐ , ☐)

B (☐ , ☐)

C (☐ , ☐)

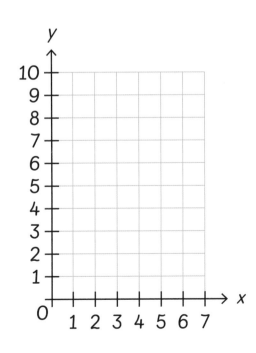

Roman numerals

Starter

Roman numerals are a number system developed in ancient Rome in which letters represent numbers. This is how the Romans wrote numerals for 1 to 20.

I	= 1	XI	= 11
II	= 2	XII	= 12
III	= 3	XIII	= 13
IV	= 4	XIV	= 14
V	= 5	XV	= 15
VI	= 6	XVI	= 16
VII	= 7	XVII	= 17
VIII	= 8	VIII	= 18
IX	= 9	XIX	= 19
X	= 10	XX	= 20

How can we write greater numbers using Roman numerals?

Example

We use the system for writing numbers 1 to 20 to work out how to write greater numbers.

II = 2   XX = 20
III = 3   XXX = 30

4 is written as 1 less than 5.
IV = 4

40 is written as 10 less than 50.
XL = 40

L is 50 so 60 is written as LX, 70 as LXX and 80 as LXXX.

Writing 10 before 100 makes 90.
XC = 90

C = 100

Practice

1 The chapter numbers in Ravi's book are written in Roman numerals. What do these Roman numerals stand for?

(a)

XIII – The Dark Night

XIII = ☐

(b)

XXIV – Here Once More

XXIV = ☐

(c)

XLVI – The End is Close

XLVI = ☐

2 Write the following numbers using Roman numerals.

(a) 88 = ☐

(b) 49 = ☐

(c) 44 = ☐

(d) 99 = ☐

Answers

Page 5   **1 (a)** 12.6 **(b)** 88 **(c)** 10.10 **(d)** 95.09 **2 (a–b)** Answers will vary. For example: 35.69, 56.93, 69.53, 95.36. **3** 2.53

Page 7   **1 (a)** 46.9 kg ≈ 47 kg **(b)** 25.1 kg ≈ 25 kg **(c)** 44.5 kg ≈ 45 kg **2 (a)** 12.7 cm ≈ 13 cm **(b)** 15.2 cm ≈ 15 cm; The total length of both strips of ribbon is approximately 28 cm.

Page 9   **1 (a)** $\frac{4}{10}$ = 4 tenths = 0.4 **(b)** $\frac{3}{4}$ = 75 hundreds = 0.75 **(c)** $\frac{2}{5}$ = 4 tenths = 0.4

2 (a) $6\frac{7}{10}$ kg = 6.7 kg **(b)** $3\frac{1}{2}$ cm = 3.5 cm **(c)** $2\frac{1}{4}$ km = 2.25 km **(d)** $7\frac{4}{5}$ kg = 7.8 kg

Page 11   **1** 9 ÷ 10 = 0.9 **2** 9 ÷ 100 = 0.09 **3** 11 ÷ 10 = 1.1 **4** 11 ÷ 100 = 0.11
5 80 ÷ 10 = 8 **6** 80 ÷ 100 = 0.8

Page 13   **1 (a)** 2345 + 10 = 2355, 2345 + 9 = 2354 **(b)** 100 + 587 = 687, 99 + 587 = 686
(c) 3269 + 500 = 3769, 3269 + 499 = 3768 **(d)** 4231 + 4000 = 8231, 4231 + 3998 = 8229
2 (a) 999 + 2999 = 3998 **(b)** 999 + 3001 = 4000 **(c)** 5997 + 998 = 6995
(d) 3998 + 5998 = 9996

Page 15   **1 (a)** 43 − 19 = 24 **(b)** 101 − 99 = 2 **(c)** 803 − 198 = 605 **(d)** 1000 − 326 = 674
(e) 5000 − 1674 = 3326 **(f)** 9008 − 99 = 8909 **2 (a)** 1001 − 999 = 2 **(b)** 1001 − 199 = 802
(c) 700 − 675 = 25 **(d)** 1700 − 1575 = 125

Page 17   **1** He bakes 525 brown bread rolls. **2** He bakes 921 bread rolls altogether.
3 Altogether, 223 bread rolls are left over.

Page 19   **1 (a)** 123 × 4 = 492 **(b)** 333 × 9 = 2997 **(c)** 835 × 6 = 5010 **(d)** 799 × 7 = 5593
2 Answers will vary. **3** Emma scored 1350 points in total over the 3 days.

Page 21   **1 (a)** 168 ÷ 4 = 42 **(b)** 861 ÷ 3 = 287 **(c)** 545 ÷ 5 = 109 **(d)** 918 ÷ 6 = 153 **2** Each person gets £17. **3** The pastry chef needs 108 boxes.

Page 23   **1 (a)** 200 ÷ 7 = 28 remainder 4 **(b)** 314 ÷ 6 = 52 remainder 2 **(c)** 567 ÷ 8 = 70 remainder 7
2 (a) Each class receives 29 pencils. **(b)** 5 pencils are left over.

Page 25   **1** 192 people are not wearing goggles. **2** Lulu can make 17 necklaces.

Page 27   **1** The waiters can fill $14\frac{2}{3}$ of the $\frac{3}{4}$ l bottles. **2** The restaurant can serve 12 customers from $4\frac{4}{5}$ pizzas.

Page 29   **1 (a)** $\frac{3}{4} + \frac{3}{4} = 1\frac{2}{4}$ OR $1\frac{1}{2}$ **(b)** $\frac{5}{8} + \frac{7}{8} = 1\frac{4}{8}$ OR $1\frac{1}{2}$ **(c)** $\frac{9}{10} + \frac{7}{10} = 1\frac{6}{10}$ OR $1\frac{3}{5}$ **(d)** $3\frac{4}{5} + 4\frac{3}{5} = 8\frac{2}{5}$

2 The two boys have $1\frac{3}{9}$ OR $1\frac{1}{3}$ chocolate bars altogether.

3 Charles has $6\frac{2}{6}$ OR $6\frac{1}{3}$ m of ribbon in total.

Page 31   **1** There is $1\frac{1}{2}$ l of water left in the jug. **2** There is $2\frac{3}{6}$ OR $2\frac{1}{2}$ l of paint left in the can.

Page 33   **1** Sam has 9 OR nine $\frac{1}{4}$ kg bags of rice. **2** Emma has $1\frac{1}{8}$ l of pineapple juice left.

3 Each friend will get $\frac{1}{6}$ of cake.

Page 35   **1** The bus journey started at 19:25. **2** Oak was away from home for 3 h 10 min.
3 Amira needs to leave home for the shopping centre at 14:55.

Page 37   **1** Area of A = 12 square units **2** Area of B = 40 square units **3** Area of C = 16 square units
4 Area of D = 18 square units **5** Area of E = 12 square units

Page 39   **1** £4.50 ≈ £5, £7.99 ≈ £8, £12.65 ≈ £13; The total cost of these items is £26 (to the nearest £).
2 (a) The total cost of the meal is £62 (to the nearest £). **(b)** ice cream

Page 41   **1**

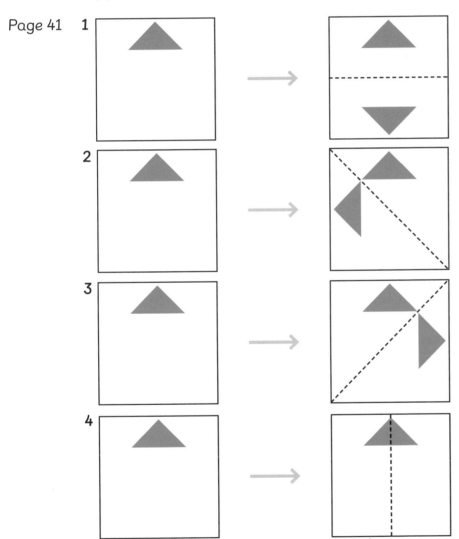

47

Answers continued

Page 43   **1 (a)** 1 unit down, 1 unit left OR 1 unit left, 1 unit down   **(b)** 1 unit up, 3 units right OR 3 unit$\cdot$ right, 1 unit up   **(c)** 2 units up, 1 unit right OR 1 unit right, 2 units up

2 (a)   **(b)**   **(c)** A (4,9), B (4,7), C (6,7)

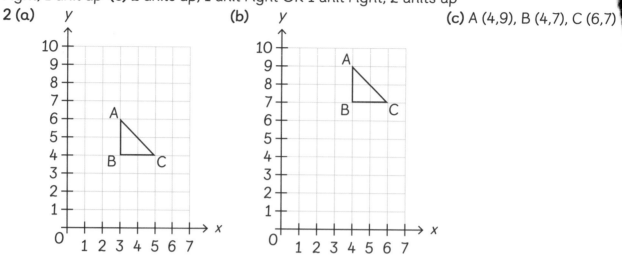

Page 45   **1 (a)** XIII = 13   **(b)** XXIV = 24   **(c)** XLVI = 46   **2 (a)** 88 = LXXXVIII   **(b)** 49 = XLIX OR IL
(c) 44 = XLIV   **(d)** 99 = XCIX OR IC